D1591148

STUDIES IN CREATIVE CRITICISM

Traditio-Historical Criticism
of the Gospels

STUDIES IN CREATIVE CRITICISM

Traditio–Historical Criticism of the Gospels

SOME COMMENTS ON CURRENT METHODS

R.S. Barbour

LONDON SPCK 1972

First published 1972
by S.P.C.K.
Holy Trinity Church
Marylebone Road
London NW1 4DU

Made and printed in Great Britain by
The Talbot Press (S.P.C.K.), Saffron Walden, Essex

SBN 281 02676 9

CONTENTS

1

No one need spend time today defending the right of scholars to apply historical-critical methods to the Gospels; but each scholar needs to spend time defending both his methods and his conclusions, for on neither of these is there anything like agreement. So far as the conclusions are concerned this is only too obvious; views of all sorts abound, and the labels "radical" and "conservative" are, unfortunately, just as emotive in the world of biblical scholarship as they are anywhere else. But in relation to historical and critical method it may not be quite so clear that there are great divergencies. People sometimes speak of the historical-critical *method* as if it were something shared by everybody, and indeed there must be assumptions and techniques that are widely shared, or scholars of differing persuasions would not be able to understand, argue with, and even sometimes convince one another as in fact they do. Nevertheless *methods* often differ widely, and it is surprising that until comparatively recent years there was, on the whole, little explicit methodological discussion among New Testament scholars. But in recent years there has been a flourishing growth in this industry also, and it is in a tiny corner of it that I am attempting to fulfil my norm here.

Students of the Gospels, as of large tracts of the Old Testament, are dealing with documents which have both an oral and a literary ancestry. The antecedent oral tradition is not necessarily prior in time to the literary; the two may have run concurrently and influenced one another (this certainly happened in the case of the Synoptic tradition, to which I confine myself here). The tracing of the process which culminated in the writing of the Gospels, as of the Pentateuch, thus requires the use of techniques which will take account of both an oral and a literary historical development; and it is to describe these techniques or methods that the phrase "traditio-historical criticism" and others like it have been coined. To survey the whole development of these techniques would be an impossible task, certainly for me; a brief reference to one aspect of the whole story is probably sufficient by way of background to what follows.

1

The development of Pentateuchal criticism especially associated with the name of Wellhausen naturally led to the conclusion that the five Books of Moses, written long after the events they purported to describe, tell us more about the period within which they were written than they do about the events themselves; and the subsequent rise of form-critical studies has in some ways reinforced that conclusion. Old Testament form-critical studies have powerfully affected the study of the New Testament where it is often also argued or assumed that the Gospels tell us more about the communities within which they were produced than about the life and teaching of Jesus which is their ostensible subject. But whereas in the case of the Old Testament the sheer distance in time between the final editing of the documents and the events described was presumably a major factor in leading to sceptical conclusions about the documents' value as historical evidence for those early events, in the case of the New Testament the gap in time is very much shorter. Here the main reason for scepticism about the amount of reliable historical information contained in the Gospels has probably been one form or another of the conviction that the Gospels are written to strengthen faith rather than to supply historical information, that they are witnesses to the Risen Lord rather than history. At all events we have now reached a position where, whether we agree with it or not, we must take seriously the view that the progress of traditio-historical criticism has called in question the historical reliability of the entire Gospel tradition. In the words of Ernst Käsemann's well-known essay on the historical Jesus:

> . . . our questioning has sharpened and widened until the obligation now laid upon us is to investigate and make credible not the possible unauthenticity of the individual unit of material but, on the contrary, its genuineness.[1]

If we are so far out of sympathy with this approach that we are prepared to accept the whole Synoptic tradition at its face value as historical evidence except where doubts are simply forced upon us, then there is scarcely any serious problem about *criteria* by which we may judge whether or not a given section of the Gospel tradition does give us accurate historical information about the life, teaching and times of Jesus. But for all the rest of us, whether or not we agree with Käsemann that the burden of proof

2

now rests on those who would assume the general historical reliability of the Synoptic Gospels and not on those who would question it, there is a real problem about criteria by which we may distinguish what is authentic and original to Jesus from what is not. Are there any such general criteria? I want to refer briefly to some of the criteria which have been used, and to consider two of them at greater length. I begin by making a rough distinction between formal and material criteria. By formal criteria I mean criteria which arise from the form in which material has been handed down or from the place which it occupies in the Gospel tradition as we now have it; by material criteria I mean criteria which have to do with the actual content of the material itself. The distinction is only a rough-and-ready one, but it has its usefulness. What follows is primarily but not entirely concerned with the sayings of Jesus; a fuller investigation would obviously have to make a more careful distinction between sayings and other material.

1. FORMAL CRITERIA[2]

As a preliminary we remind ourselves that we cannot safely use the mere fact that a saying is handed down as a saying of the earthly Jesus as a formal criterion of its genuineness. It is a widespread assumption today that early Christian prophets, speaking in the name of Christ, pronounced oracles which came to be accepted as sayings of the earthly Jesus, and that the early Church made no distinction between these words of the Risen Lord and genuine sayings of the earthly Jesus. This assumption seems to me to be very questionable, in the form in which I have stated it; but even so it would not be safe to assume that there are no "sayings of the Risen Lord" included in pre-Resurrection contexts in our Gospels. "Where two or three are gathered in my name, there am I in the midst of them" (Matt. 18.20) seems an obvious example. Are there then any other formal criteria by which we can distinguish what Jesus actually said and did?

I now mention four such formal criteria (of slightly differing kinds, but all relevant to our later discussion) which have been used to distinguish original material in the Gospels:

a. Multiple attestation
Where a saying of Jesus, or more often a general characteristic

3

of his teaching or conduct, is vouched for in more than one, or in all our main sources (Mark, Q, the special Matthew material, the special Luke material, according to the prevalent hypothesis) there would appear to be a strong case for saying that it is original, especially if such sources can be shown to have been originally independent of one another. Jesus' consorting with tax-collectors and "sinners" is a case in point.[3] On this I would only comment that while it is obviously a most useful criterion, it is not by itself a safe one;[4] the more radical critic is only likely to accept it where, as a formal criterion, it can be joined with a material one; i.e., (and we shall come to this later) where the words or actions of Jesus concerned show a distinctiveness over against his environment that gives them a further claim to origina- lity. There are many varieties of this criterion—a good example of one of them is to be found in C. H. Dodd's *History and the Gospel*, pp. 91–101—which we must here pass over.

b. Aramaisms, and other signs of an origin within Palestinian Judaism
These are presumably an important, but not a sufficient condition of genuineness, since material that on other grounds could be ascribed to the earliest Palestinian Church, or to contemporary Judaism, will also be likely to exhibit them. A specially important form of this second criterion is

c. Poetic form and parallelism within the logia Jesu.
Here again the purely formal criterion only demonstrates Pales- tinian origin, and must be supplemented by other accrediting features, such as distinctiveness of content. It is worth noticing in passing that this criterion has been much in evidence in recent assessment of the *logia* found in the Gospel of Thomas.[5]

d. No doubt there are other formal criteria which could be or have been used to distinguish genuine words of Jesus. Sometimes the judgement seems to be almost an intuitive one: thus for example William Manson wrote of Mark 9.12 ("How is it written with regard to the Son of Man? That he must suffer many things, and be set at nought") that it "has the rugged and irreducible form of an original oracle".[6] (To say that a judgement is intuitive is by no means to condemn it—whether or not the use of the word is fair to Manson here. Creative intuitions lead to creative

4

hypotheses, in Gospel study as in scientific method.) Or again, from certain points of view one could say that Jesus' use of *Amen* to preface his declarations, and of *Abba* to address his Father, can be taken as formal criteria of originality. But in most of these cases the formal and the material aspects of the criterion are inseparable. We might therefore have some sympathy with Käsemann, even if we think he is exaggerating, when he says in the article already cited that "apart from the parables we possess absolutely no kind of formal criteria by which we can identify the authentic Jesus material".[7] Formal criteria by themselves have only a very limited usefulness.

Käsemann goes on to claim that "the case is not markedly different if we take as criteria the primitive Christian chronology or the actual content of what is set forth. . . it is just the earliest phase of all, upon the comparison of which with the Jesus tradition everything might well depend, which remains absolutely opaque to us, particularly as regards its soteriology and ecclesiology" (p. 36). "In only one case do we have more or less safe ground under our feet; where there are no grounds either for deriving a tradition from Judaism or for ascribing it to primitive Christianity, and especially when Jewish Christianity has mitigated or modified the received tradition, as having found it too bold for its taste" (p. 37). Here, it seems to me, many awkward questions raise their heads; but these criteria have been widely adopted in recent study,[8] and with them we pass from the formal to the material criteria which are our main concern.

2. MATERIAL CRITERIA

Käsemann's two criteria for genuineness are briefly applied in the following section of his article, entitled "the distinctive element in the teaching of Jesus", with results which will be familiar to many of us. We should notice in passing that he does not confine the applicability of these criteria to the sayings of Jesus, although he does specifically exclude the parables, presumably because they are, in content if not always in form, so obviously distinctive to Jesus himself that the methods of form criticism as applied to them by Jeremias and others can lead us back not only to an original form but to their original situation and meaning within the ministry of Jesus itself. Another statement of these principles, however, from the pen of R. H. Fuller[9] explicitly confines its reference to the sayings of Jesus and does not exclude the parables. Fuller writes:

> As regards the sayings of Jesus, traditio-historical criticism eliminates from the authentic sayings of Jesus those which are paralleled in the Jewish tradition on the one hand (apocalyptic and Rabbinic) and those which reflect the faith, practice and situations of the post-Easter church as we know them from outside the Gospels.

This statement is to say the least unguarded (although Fuller does present the matter rather more cautiously elsewhere). At least four criticisms are immediately obvious. In the first place, these criteria appear to conflict with the demand already mentioned (and accepted by Fuller) that what is genuine should be consistent with a background in first-century Palestinian Judaism. Material is to be eliminated if it *can* be paralleled in contemporary Judaism, and also if it has a background which *cannot* be positively shown to be consistent with Palestinian Judaism of the first century. No wonder it is said that our knowledge of the historical Jesus is scanty; it is all eliminated before we start. Of course that cannot be what is meant. Perhaps we can crawl out of this difficulty by distinguishing again between the formal and the material. Sayings of Jesus, or other pieces of the tradition, which exhibit *formal* characteristics that are consistent with Palestinian first-century Judaism—poetic parallelism etc.—but have a content that is distinctive *can* claim genuineness or originality. We may accept this defence for the moment, while agreeing with another recent writer that "there seem to be enormous possibilities for confusion" here.[10]

But secondly, we must make a protest at Fuller's statement that material which fails to pass this test is to be *eliminated* from the authentic sayings of Jesus. What he must surely mean is that the sayings, etc, which pass this test give us, in Nils Dahl's phrase, "a critically assured minimum".[11] As Dr Morna Hooker remarks in the introduction to her book *The Son of Man in Mark:*

> If we place a saying or tradition to the *credit* of the Church, are we necessarily obliged to *debit* it from our picture of Jesus?
> . . . . To reduce the number of "authentic" *logia* to such an extent may produce a picture of Jesus which is so unbalanced

as to be misleading, for we shall have eliminated not only later accretions, but also the material which could possibly be common to Jesus and the Church, and which may explain the continuity between them (pp. 6f.).

What Dr Hooker says about material which is to be eliminated because it reflects the concerns of the early Church can and must obviously also be said, *mutatis mutandis,* about material which could have come from contemporary Judaism. There must have been a continuity at many points between Jesus and his contemporaries in Palestine.

Thirdly, it is worth observing at this stage that even if these methods or criteria under discussion are valid in other respects, the success of their use depends on the extent of our knowledge of the two areas with which the tradition about Jesus is to be compared and contrasted, namely contemporary Judaism and the early Church. Our knowledge of the earliest days of the Church is sketchy and partial; disconcerting as this may be for modern scholars, it was clearly not necessary for salvation that a thorough historical knowledge of all the main trends and movements in the early Church should be available to us. Something the same is true of Judaism in the first century; our picture of it today is enormously extended and diversified by comparison with that of previous generations, but it is still very far from being comprehensive. In using these criteria we must therefore proceed quite tentatively; all we can say is that in the present state of our knowledge things look like this.

Part of the trouble here probably is that people are too easily deceived into thinking that our knowledge of the early Church is somehow direct or unmediated whereas our knowledge of the historical Jesus is mediated or filtered through the multi-coloured spectacles of the early Church. In fact, no historical knowledge of any kind is direct or unmediated, and for certain purposes at any rate we must cease speaking as if, in passing from the early Church back to the figure of Jesus, we are moving from a known to an unknown; rather we are moving from one partially known to another partially known. Questions of historical method and issues in the philosophy of history are raised here which it would be very relevant to pursue, and one or two of them are touched on below.

A fourth difficulty about the criteria we are discussing is that they are extremely difficult to apply: what constitutes a relevant parallel in contemporary Judaism or in the belief and practice of the early Church? What constitutes distinctiveness or uniqueness in the ministry of Jesus? To take two quick examples:

a. It used to be said that the bringing together of the two great commandments of love for God and for the neighbour (Mk. 12. 28–34 and parallels) as a single summary of God's law was due to Jesus. Recent study suggests that in fact this may not have been so.[12] Are we going to turn round and say we can no longer assert that Jesus in fact brought these two commandments together simply because it now seems likely that Judaism had already done so and that Jesus' teaching was not at this point distinctive or original? The way in which Jesus brought them together (if he did in fact do so); the exegesis which he gave to the commandment of love for the neighbour (if for example the parable of the Good Samaritan is to be treated as "exegesis" of that commandment); the context in which he did this—all these things are relevant before any judgement on originality is possible. The question of distinctiveness or originality cannot be considered in relation to sayings of Jesus, *perikopae* in the Gospels, or aspects of his teaching *in isolation.*

b. Jesus' use of *Amen* to preface certain of his declarations has already been mentioned. It is commonly held to be without parallel in contemporary Judaism, although David Daube has drawn attention to some possible partial approximations to it. But in any case a remark with which Daube prefaces his discussion is worth quoting here:

> Whoever introduced the "Amen" under discussion. . . must have relied on some support in contemporary speech or in a special tradition. He could not have brought in the new use of "Amen", as it were, *ex nihilo.* If he had, it would have produced no effect.[13]

The wholly unique would be the totally incomprehensible.

Many more points could of course be made. I hope that the two examples above illustrate two of the difficulties in applying the criteria we are discussing. That is not to deny their usefulness, but merely to point out what is surely sufficiently obvious, that they are difficult tools to use with any precision.

No doubt the scholars we have mentioned, and others, are aware of the points just made, although there is still room for complaint, I think, that they do not always express their awareness as clearly as they might.

In his recent work *Rediscovering the Teaching of Jesus* Norman Perrin puts together the two heuristic principles we have been discussing and labels them the "criterion of dissimilarity" (p. 39). What is dissimilar, in the tradition about Jesus, from his Jewish background and from the characteristic faith-attitudes—call them what you will—of the early Church can be proposed as genuine material. Realizing that this does in fact provide no more than a critically assured minimum Perrin then goes on to propose another criterion which he calls the "criterion of coherence" (p. 43).[14] What is *coherent with* the material accepted as genuine by means of the criterion of dissimilarity can also be accepted as genuine. We may agree that some use of a criterion of this kind is inevitable and right. But again difficulties immediately occur. By what standard are we to judge coherence? What seems coherent to the modern scholar or historian or theologian may not have seemed coherent to the first-century Jew or Christian; and what now seems incoherent may not have seemed incoherent then. Discussing predestination in the New Testament, Krister Stendahl has written:

> Predestination causes difficulty because it is also necessary to assert man's responsibility. But man's responsibility is a paradox when placed beside any meaningful doctrine of election. Clearly the New Testament writers did not feel this difficulty in the same way as later theologians. Here again we can contrast two ways of thinking. Over against stringent logic stands Jewish thinking in images, where contradictory facts and conceptions can be put together in a kind of significant mosaic. Because of the peculiar character of Jewish thinking, the incompatibility of election and personal responsibility does not give rise to an intellectual problem in the New Testament.[15]

As with the New Testament writers and Jews of the day, so presumably with Jesus (or must he have been distinctive here too?). We must not apply irrelevant criteria of coherence to Jesus' teaching as we find it, for example, throughout the Gospel of Matthew. Here already we see a case where instinctively we tend

9

to reject the criterion of dissimilarity in favour of a presumption of *similarity* between Jesus, his contemporaries and his immediate followers. If he was a Jew, he presumably thought like a Jew. Quite clearly a whole constellation of hermeneutical, not to say christological, questions immediately arises here. This is not to deny all usefulness to some form of criterion of coherence, without which scholarly study would be impossible, but to give a preliminary warning about the difficulty in using it. In particular, we must not assume that Jesus' teaching will necessarily appear *to us* as a single coherent whole—a point of very great relevance in the whole tangled discussion about the Son of Man, and one made forcefully by one of the most recent writers on the subject, F. H. Borsch.[16]

Perrin makes a further point and thereby adds another criterion for assessing what is original to Jesus:

> If we are to establish any sayings attributed to Jesus in the tradition as authentic, then the first thing we must be able to do is to write a history of the tradition of which a given saying is a part, establishing so far as we are able to do so the earliest form of the saying known in the tradition.[17]

This may seem so obvious as not to need any mention; it is implied in the phrase "traditio-historical criticism", and might seem to be the most prominent feature of the whole effort of recent Gospel research. But it is doubtful whether many contemporary authors really carry their principle through. If the criteria we have been discussing, and others which we have not been able to discuss have any validity, they have it in the context of the attempt to write the whole history of the tradition; that is, in the context of the framing of hypotheses which will seek to account as adequately as possible for all the literary and historical phenomena. But all too often what happens is something like this. If a writer's main interest is in the original teaching of Jesus (as is Perrin's in the book just quoted) he uses his heuristic criteria to isolate what he considers to be genuine, and the rest he puts aside without a full examination of the likelihood of their being secondary constructions or prophetic utterances of the early Church. The belief, which is doubtless correct, that most of the material in the synoptic Gospels has a *Sitz im Leben* in the concerns of the early Church and is not simply remembered because

Jesus said it or did it and for no other reason, is turned into the different and much more questionable assumption that because the material has a *Sitz im Leben* in the early Church, therefore the early Church may plausibly be assumed to have composed it. The point here is not simply the one already noted, that to find a *Sitz im Leben* within the early Church does not imply that there was no original word or act of Jesus; the point is the equally obvious one that the genesis of sayings deemed unoriginal must be accounted for just as fully as the genesis of sayings deemed original, before they suffer an exodus on to the scrap-heap of the secondary. (Not that the secondary is valueless for an understanding of Jesus—but to discuss that would take us too far afield.) I do not think that anyone who has read much recent literature on this subject can deny that the sort of thing I have been trying to describe sometimes happens.

Often no positive account of the genesis of material deemed secondary is given at all; sometimes what is given is very jejune.[18] Further, if a positive account is given, and appears convincing, with regard to a single saying or series of sayings or other block of material, it still has to be fitted into a satisfactory over-all picture or made to conform with a general hypothesis— the criterion of coherence is relevant here as everywhere, however difficult it may be to apply.

To take a broad example: some scholars who have written on the Son of Man within the last decade have come to the conclusion that *all* or almost all the Son of Man sayings in the Gospels are secondary or church formulations. In this connection the names of Philipp Vielhauer, [19] Hans Conzelmann,[20] and Howard M. Teeple[21] come to mind. For such theories to be plausible several conditions would have to be fulfilled, among them being that: *i.* the genesis of each Son of Man saying can be convincingly accounted for and its development, if any, thereafter traced; *ii.* its present position in the Gospels can be convincingly accounted for; *iii.* the whole can be fitted into an overall hypothesis which can at least claim to be worth consideration. Of course the same is true about any theory concerning the Son of Man sayings, and the whole issue is intractable just because no fully convincing theory has yet been produced. In relation to the authors just mentioned I think we must say that: *i.* they have not in general paid enough attention to the question why differing strands of the tradition contain different types of Son of Man saying, how they are related, and why each came to be incorporated into its present context; and in particular that they have not examined the possible motives for the alleged development of Son of Man sayings with sufficient care; *ii.* their general accounts of the situation within which this massive development of post-Resurrection Son of Man sayings is alleged to have taken place are seriously deficient if not misleading at a number of points. What type of creative process was it, operating under what constraining influences, that produced after Easter all these sayings about the Son of Man, all in the third person, some apparently distinguishing the Son of Man from Jesus himself, all on Jesus' lips (save John 12.34), none combining "I" (*ego*) with the Son of Man (this reading in Matthew 16.13 is certainly secondary), statements ranging over a variety of themes, and very varied in form? What kind of sensitivity was it that prevented such sayings from being placed on the disciples' lips, but had no scruples about their being placed on the lips of Jesus? I do not find these questions and others like them sufficiently, or sufficiently convincingly, answered in the writings of the scholars in question: although, as I have already said, there is no possibility now of pursuing the issue in detail; and there, unfortunately, we must for the moment leave the large question of the Son of Man.[22]

I have been criticizing those who fail to give adequate explanations of the origin of material they consider secondary. It is only fair to add that in many cases quite the reverse is true. Another quick example: two German scholars, G. Klein and Miss Eta Linnemann, have recently made detailed studies of the story of Peter's denial in which they reach the conclusion (which to me appears highly improbable) that the story is not historical. But at least they offer careful accounts of the supposed *Sitz im Leben* of the tradition in the early Church; and this is better than simply describing it as "literary", "legendary", and "novelistic" (Bultmann).[23] It is only fair also to add that similar remarks apply to material which is considered to be original to Jesus himself. The question of its origin is not simply settled by ascribing it to Jesus: the problem of the context of such sayings or incidents, of what they originally meant, of their place in Jesus' message or teaching, arises and must be dealt with. No doubt it would be possible to cite instances of failure to do this just as it is possible to cite instances in the case of those who assign material to the creativity of the early Church. But again, we cannot elaborate details in a short study.

A rather sterile argument about criteria has sometimes arisen here between those who maintain that individuals and not communities are creative, so that arresting and original material in the Gospels is *pro tanto* likely to come from Jesus himself and not from the anonymous womb of the early community, and those who use the arguments of form criticism to show that the Gospels are *Kleinliteratur*, the products of a communal oral tradition. The argument has in fact been sterile because there has been too little accurate investigation of the principles adduced: is it in fact true, or is it not true, in different epochs and civilizations, that communities are creative? But, more important, the terms are not sufficiently defined: what does it mean to say that communities are or are not creative? The practice of anonymity, the processes of imaginative creation within an oral tradition, and many other factors are relevant here. Further study may lead to clearer conclusions than can be reached at the moment. But in the meantime it is instructive to notice how those scholars who are readiest to ascribe distinctive or unique individual characteristics to Jesus—his directness in utterance, his cutting through all respect for authority to proclaim the Will of God directly, and so forth—appear sometimes to be the least ready to allow him any originality in theological synthesis, in reassessment of the Old Testament as a whole, and in general in reflective activities of the same kind as the early Church undoubtedly carried on. This may be due to the nature of the sources; it may also be due to the type of historical criteria used to evaluate them.

3. MESSIANIC BELIEFS AND HISTORICAL CRITERIA

The criteria which we have mentioned so far have been almost entirely of a general kind; they might apply in widely varying historical circumstances, and they would have a use outside the area of Christian origins, even if their use within this area has certain special features. One might use them in relation to any great teacher who left no writings of his own and round whom

13

an extensive tradition grew up. As we have seen, they are used in particular by scholars for whom historical criticism has thrown the reliability of the Synoptic tradition into doubt all along the line. A major feature of such doubt has been the doubt whether Jesus claimed for himself, either openly or privately, any of the Messianic titles traditionally supposed to have been claimed by him. Especially influential here has been the work of Wilhelm Wrede which threw the spotlight on the title "Messiah" and sought to show that Jesus had made no Messianic claim and had not been hailed as Messiah either by the disciples or by others before the Resurrection. This conclusion would lead to the formulation of the heuristic criterion: "any material which states or implies that Jesus claimed or was claimed to be the Messiah during his ministry is a production of the early Church". Such criteria—which are in effect hypotheses rather than criteria—are, of course, frequently used not only in regard to the title Messiah but also in regard to the other christological titles. One theme or title affects another: the radical *Son of Man* theories have surely gained some of their plausibility from the assumption that Jesus made no claims to the title *Messiah*. Of course there is no unanimity here. All the following positions, and a number of others, have been held in the last few years: Jesus claimed and was given no Messianic titles during his lifetime; he spoke of himself as Son of Man in one or more of several senses of the term but did not claim to be Messiah; he was hailed as Messiah and accused of making the claim although he had not done so; he openly claimed Messiahship at his trial; he claimed to embody the fulfilment of the Isaianic servant prophecies; he did not make this claim etc., etc. In all this confusion of hypotheses the view has gained ground that while Jesus did not explicitly claim Messianic titles he did make claims, whether implicit or explicit, which were just as far-reaching as the Messianic claims and perhaps much more so.

Now how far has all this resulted from the use of the criteria we have been considering, and in particular the two criteria which are known together as the criterion of dissimilarity? We have noticed already the statement of Nils Dahl that what this criterion gives us is "a critically assured minimum"; what we now have to remember is the obvious fact that it gives us a delimitation of that minimum in terms of what is distinctive of

Jesus over against his surroundings in space and time. Those respects in which he was not distinctive are likely to be excluded from the "critically assured minimum portrait" (I say "likely to be" rather than "certain to be" both because no scholar in fact applies a criterion of this kind with complete rigour and because a certain amount of "non-distinctive" matter is bound to slip through the net even when it is being used as rigorously as possible). But that means that we are *a priori* likely to exclude *both* those features of his teaching which were typical of the surrounding Judaism *and* those Messianic claims (if there were any) which would certainly be distinctive, although not unique, from the point of view of his Jewish contemporaries but did not distinguish him from his early Christian followers. The use of the criterion of dissimilarity seems likely to give us a Jesus who presents a very distinctive figure, but not in the way in which the early Christian community regarded him as distinctive; who makes great claims, but not in terms of the titles which form the framework of early Christology. It is therefore likely to make the problem of continuity between the Jesus of history and the Christ of faith, about which the new questers of the historical Jesus are naturally so concerned, extremely difficult to solve except by means of a *tertium comparationis* like the concept of *Existenzverständnis* (understanding of existence), eschatological urgency, or something of the kind which can be found in both halves of the equation. (It is just here, incidentally, that the term Son of Man is so important, because it appears very frequently on the lips of Jesus in the Gospels but never in the New Testament in a narrowly doxological, kerygmatic, or credal context; it does not yield, therefore, to the same kind of treatment that has been applied to other titles which admittedly are used in such contexts.)

No doubt it is true, in spite of Kierkegaard's incognito, that Jesus was a highly distinctive figure; but we do nothing to exalt his distinctiveness by setting up criteria which come near to prescribing its nature before we have started, and this is what the recent application of this criterion of dissimilarity seems in danger of doing. Perrin, e.g., says that "if we are to seek that which is most characteristic of Jesus, it will be found not in the things which he shares with his contemporaries, but in the things wherein he differs from them".[24] Now apart from the vagueness of a phrase like "that which is most characteristic of Jesus" (some meanings of it would make the sentence quoted a tautology) it is begging the question to say at the start of the investigation that this quality will be found not in the things which Jesus shared with his contemporaries but in the things where he differed from them. One suspects a hidden presupposition here somewhat along these lines: The historical Jesus' person and work must be shown to be unique; that uniqueness cannot be expressed in terms of the titles ascribed to him by early Christianity, because these are all under suspicion as being later ascriptions; therefore it must be expressed in terms which are not impregnated with Christology, i.e., in terms of the distinctive or unique things he said and did which were not explicitly christologically oriented. The fundamental presupposition is partly historical, partly christological or apologetic in character. Before we examine it a little further we should notice that it could be expressed in a rather more general form than that which I have used, by substituting the word "kerygmatic" for the word "Christological": "the historical Jesus' uniqueness cannot be expressed in kerygmatic terms because these are under suspicion as being later ascriptions; therefore it must be expressed in terms of the unique or distinctive things he said and did which were not of a kerygmatic character". But while this formulation might satisfy some scholars, it would hardly satisfy others. J. M. Robinson, for example, sees a new possibility for uncovering the historical Jesus arising precisely out of the fact that the Gospels have preserved historical material in a kerygmatic form.

> The kind of material which the "kerygmatizing" process would leave *unaltered* [he writes] is the kind of material which fits best the needs of research based upon the modern view of history and the self. For the kerygmatic interest of the primitive Church would leave unaltered precisely those sayings and scenes in which Jesus made his intention and understanding of existence most apparent to them.[25]

Thus, as is familiar, he finds a way back to the historical Jesus through that form of modern historiography which discovers that Jesus' understanding of existence was similar to its own. For us, however, the point is simply that here is a case where a criterion of similarity rather than dissimilarity is used; but, be it noted, this is only so because an external standard has been brought in to act as a *tertium comparationis:* the concept of an understanding of existence; and later in his book (pp. 104ff) Robinson argues that the way back to Jesus which bypasses the kerygma is in certain respects superior to the other.

It is perhaps worth while at this point to reflect for a moment on the success of the argument of Joachim Jeremias (now found most easily in *The Prayers of Jesus*) about Jesus' use of the familiar vocative form *Abba* in prayer to the Father. (This can operate, as we saw, both as a formal and as a material criterion of genuineness.) The essential part of the proof of its genuineness as a characteristic of the *ipsissima vox Jesu* consists in showing that it is distinctive to Jesus; nowhere else in the vast literature of Judaism is *Abba* found as an address to God. It is of course as characteristic of the prayers of the early Church as one could wish; furthermore, it is rare in the earlier strata of the tradition; and it might seem natural, especially since we are here dealing with worship, to assume that it is a product of the early Church's spontaneous sense of sonship, a sonship which of course the early Christians also ascribed *sensu eminenti* to Jesus himself. But of course few if any have drawn this conclusion. Why? Probably largely because the use of *Abba* is neither christological in the narrow sense—to do with the titles of Jesus—nor kerygmatic—to do with the proclamation of the Gospel. Thus although the second part of the criterion of dissimilarity might seem to tell against its genuineness, the use of Abba has come to be almost universally accepted as an original, and most revealing, feature of the language of Jesus. (Whether and how far it can be a basis for a Christology is another matter.)

I take this example simply to illustrate the suggestion that this criterion of dissimilarity has attained the broad currency which it enjoys not so much because it is a particularly helpful historical tool but more because it is a consequence of certain apologetic assumptions. Jeremias' argument about the distinctiveness, and therefore the genuineness, of the word *Abba* on the lips of Jesus is convincing not simply because it is in agreement with the criterion of "dissimilarity from the Jewish background", but also because we do not suspect creative activity on the part of the early Church nearly so easily where neither the *kerygma* nor the Messianic titles of Jesus are directly involved.[26]

A further point about the use of the criteria we have been

discussing will lead to the next section. These and other similar methods tend to make us divide the material about Jesus into two rather rigid categories, the genuine or authentic or original, and the secondary or inauthentic (not to say spurious), which is the creation of the Church. Of course everybody realizes that there is a third category of material which is neither exactly the one nor the other, but which has undergone some form of modification within the tradition. But far too often the possibility —indeed virtual certainty—that the third category is a large one is not taken seriously enough; a fact which has been particularly evident in the debates about the Son of Man sayings. Apart from this danger, however, it has to be noticed that a method which tends to take sayings or *perikopae* one by one, applying criteria of authenticity to each in turn, is almost certain to distort the historical picture. The form-critical method may have succeeded in showing that the bulk of the Synoptic Gospels consists of units which were originally handed down separately; but that does not imply that they can be divided into authentic and inauthentic units, as we have just seen. Nor can they be handled one by one and dropped into the appropriate boxes, as the use of criteria like that of dissimilarity almost inevitably tends to suggest. If an individual saying or *perikope* has to be handled in that way, so be it; but the provisional result always has to be integrated into an overall hypothesis, and such hypotheses are almost certain to soften the sharp edges of distinction produced by the methods under discussion.

This is not to say that all efforts to isolate a "critically assured minimum" of genuine material about Jesus, be it large or small, are necessarily mistaken; but rather to question whether the methods currently in use among many scholars are as satisfactory as can be found, and whether this isolation of a core of genuine material is in fact the first step to take. On the latter point, it would seem that there is no way round the laborious process of formulating hypotheses and testing them by all available means. If the hypothesis of a generation ago, which saw the kernel and origin of the Christian message in the bringing together of the Old Testament conceptions of Messiah, Son of Man, and Suffering Servant of the Lord in the mind of Jesus himself, has been found wanting—as I think in certain respects it has—then there is no alternative to the formulation of a modified hypothesis,

18

which in itself will be one of the determinants of what the "critically assured minimum" of genuine material actually is. At the same time techniques for isolating such a critically assured minimum will affect the formulation of hypotheses. There is no way of escape from the so-called "hermeneutical circle"—the understanding of a whole from its parts, and of the parts in the light of the whole.[27] For the use of the criterion of dissimilarity as a basic tool is not just a heuristic method, as seems to be supposed, but is in itself the adoption of an hypothesis about the historical Jesus and his relation to the early tradition, and it is worthwhile to think a little further about what sort of an hypothesis it is. It would be illuminating to do this in some detail by reference to the work of those scholars who make use of it, but since this would take a great deal of space and time I only take up two questions in the following sections, prefaced by an introductory comment.

The essence of the method is to build on what distinguishes Jesus from his surroundings—the respects in which he is distinctive or unique. In one sense of the term, every historical figure is unique—no two persons in history are wholly alike. In a second, stronger, sense of the term an historical figure may be called unique because his teachings, his actions, or his influence were of great importance and are hard to parallel. In a third, the strongest, sense, Jesus to Christian faith was (and is) unique because in him God and man speak with one voice, act together, are one. To this there is no parallel in history, as there is no parallel in history to the event (if it be an event) of the Resurrection. According to some views, such a kind or degree of uniqueness excludes all possibility of historical investigation; fortunately we need not attempt to tackle that question now. Relevant for us is the observation that the delineation of Jesus' proclamation and mission in terms of the second kind of uniqueness referred to above, which is characteristic of Bultmann's pupils, can mean that Jesus' Jewishness, his likeness to his brothers, is undervalued, his impact too simply construed, his strangeness and his incognito too easily overcome; it can also mean that the course of his human obedience, the testings and struggles, and the involvement in human affairs which must constitute a large part of the historical significance of any human figure are undervalued by contrast with the eschatological message of his teachings and conduct. We shall return to these points in the next section. But further, when we move over from uniqueness in the second sense to uniqueness in the third sense; when Jesus' remarkable demands and claims and in particular his claim to authority directly derived from, or even the same as, that of God Himself are made the basis of Christology, then the use of the criterion of dissimilarity can have very far-reaching theological effects. To aspects of that second question we shall turn in part 2 of this essay.

4. CONTEMPORARY PORTRAITS OF JESUS

We have noted already that we would expect Jesus to share the presuppositions of his day on what we now call the problem of free will and predestination; and of course the same would apply to many other realms of thought and practice. Without the assumption that he was a Jew of the first century A.D., with all that that implies, historical investigation cannot proceed; and a good deal of modern Christology can be read as an effort, for historical and theological reasons, to take that assumption, and to take the humanity of Jesus, seriously. Eutyches, as D. M. Baillie said,[28] is dead; and some have gone on, more questionably perhaps, to point out that Cyril of Alexandria and the Chalcedonian fathers are dead too. But the criterion of dissimilarity might become a tool, not indeed for exhuming some of those figures, but for burying the humanity, and especially the Jewishness, of Jesus. For if all we can know for certain about Jesus is what sets him off from his background as a unique figure, he is in some danger of becoming, as the Baptist claimed to be in the Gospel of John, a voice in the wilderness: an eschatological voice in the wilderness of history, audible at all moments within history, proclaiming the end of history it may be, the bearer of a kerygma which is kerygma precisely because it liberates men from the historical surroundings which enslave them. This may seem an absurdly sweeping judgement on something so prosaic as a criterion; and I would indeed like to think that it is. But consider for a moment the moving and eloquent picture of Jesus which Ernst Käsemann gave in the closing pages of his essay on "The Problem of the Historical Jesus" referred to earlier. Jesus speaks, he says, as one who sets himself above Moses; who in pursuit of the will of God shatters the law, both the Sabbath commandment and all the prescriptions for ceremonial purity; whose sovereign freedom "shakes the very foundations of Judaism and causes his death" (p. 40; note the assignation of a historical cause for the death of Jesus); who is more, and much more, than a prophet; who probably never claimed to be Messiah, but if he did not "it would be extraordinarily characteristic of him. He would have differentiated himself equally from late Jewish expectation and from the proclamation of his own community" (p. 44).[29] But this conclusion was already contained in the premises; a rigid application of the "criterion of dissimilarity" means precisely that what we know about Jesus is that he differentiated himself from late Jewish expectation and from the proclamation of his own community. Readers of Bornkamm's *Jesus of Nazareth* will recognize a similar—and similarly impressive—picture of Jesus there.

We must remember that Käsemann was writing of what he called "the distinctive element in the mission of Jesus", and what he gave was avowedly not complete (although he was setting out what seemed to him essential, p. 37). But it is noticeable that in this picture there is nothing about Jesus' impatience at the faithlessness of his generation, his belief in demons, his miracles, or his prophecies of woe and his proclamation of judgement; about inability to work mighty deeds where there is no faith; about suffering and the Son of Man; about the testing in the wilderness, about Gethsemane and any cry from the cross; about any change or development in the life of Jesus. All that material is either not distinctive or suspect on other grounds. And taken individually, *logion* by *logion*, *perikope* by *perikope*, it may perhaps, much of it, plausibly be held to be under some suspicion for one reason or another. But taken together it constitutes a witness to the painful course of Jesus' obedience to the Father which on general historical grounds it would be hard to reject (strong as would be our theological or apologetic motives for wanting to retain it). If the Gospels are products of the faith of the early Church, as of course in many senses they are, it is remarkable that the figure they portray has so much of righteous indignation, of hesitation in the face of suffering, of kenosis about him. Käsemann's and Bornkamm's delineations of the mission of Jesus do not have very much to say about that whole side of the picture; but without it the balance is certainly different from that of the Synoptic

Gospels as a whole; and, be it noted, in the direction of a less unmistakeably *historical* figure. For without *some* reference to possible change and development, to action and reaction between Jesus and the individuals and groups whom he encounters, it is doubtful whether a modern secular historian would recognize a properly historical figure at all—by which of course I mean not a figure who existed in history but a figure of whose existence and significance some historical account can be given.

I have dared to speak of the course of Jesus' human obedience to the Father—less daringly of course than the writer of the Epistle to the Hebrews, who says that he *learned* obedience by the things which he suffered, and in saying so does not appear to be referring solely to the trial and crucifixion. Here again we see a feature of the portrait of Jesus which is characteristic of those who use the avenue of approach we have been discussing; it is essentially the message, or more widely the words, of Jesus which fill the picture. This has been decisively noted by Hugh Anderson in his comments on Bornkamm's book.[30] Nor does Ernst Fuchs, with his emphasis on Jesus' conduct, really take up a different point of view in this regard; for him Jesus' conduct is still essentially what *speaks* to us across the centuries as something unique about him, and what we can know about him historically is what is most distinctive about his conduct. The Jesus who is brought before us by these methods proclaims, and indeed embodies, if only proleptically, the Kingdom of God; but it is not essential to the picture that he passes through that testing which enables him in the deepest human sense to be described as man, that wrestling with and taking the measure of the depth of evil in human affairs which is surely not just a theological assumption but an ineradicable historical element in the whole story as the Gospels tell it. Of course this judgement *qua* historical judgement needs a defence which cannot here be given it— a defence which would be closely connected with a re-examination of all the material about Jesus' sonship as well as with the concept of martyrdom and the suffering of the righteous one in Israel— perhaps recalling William Manson's great treatment of this whole theme in *Jesus the Messiah*. For the moment we must content ourselves with the observation that this concentration on the words or the proclamation of Jesus is partly due to the terms in which these scholars have posed their problem or had it posed for them. It is not simply that they are looking for a continuity between the proclamation of Jesus about the Kingdom of God and the proclamation of the Church about Jesus, in a situation where they believe that continuity to have become questionable; it is that in varying degrees and ways they all believe that the real Christ is the preached Christ, and they all want to link this Word of the Gospel directly to, if not to ground it theologically in, the Word of Jesus spoken long ago.

But of course those scholars who have just been characterized as laying too exclusive a stress on the words of Jesus do say in differing ways that Jesus' being is enclosed in his words, that his teaching reveals the mystery of his being, and so forth; nor are they afraid, sometimes, to speak of his self-consciousness: thus Conzelmann writes "the unity of [Jesus'] world of thought can only become visible from the perspective of his self-consciousness".[31] This "being" of Jesus that his words disclose is usually described in terms of some characteristic of the picture of Jesus as these scholars discern it—his unique eschatological self-consciousness which leaves no room for any person or event to intervene between him and the Kingdom (Conzelmann); his placing of himself, and acting, in God's stead (Fuchs); his certainty of faith (Ebeling); or, to go for a moment outside the ranks of the theologians, his unprecedented revolutionary spiritual truthfulness (Karl Jaspers); his remarkable freedom (van Buren and others); his complete openness to others (J. A. T. Robinson). (Many of these formulations raise the question: "but how could we ever know, from historical evidence, that he was *completely* or *perfectly* free for others, open to others, or for that matter free from sin?" And the answer must always be: "from historical evidence we could never know it, though historical evidence might be held to contradict it; that kind of apparently 'pure' historical judgement is always in the end a postulate of faith". But that is not the question at issue at the moment.) Even if some of the abovementioned features of his life are apparently concerned with what he did rather than what he said, with the course of his human life rather than with his message as such, they have in fact more to do with the *portrait* of him as a remarkable, indeed unique, historical figure than with an historical assessment of the work he performed and the life he lived. The picture of Jesus has, so to speak, no depth in time—and consequently a curious lack of variegation in other respects too. Partly, no doubt, that is due to a proper reaction to Hegelian portraits of Jesus which described a process of growth for which there is no satisfactory evidence; it is more directly due to the findings of form-criticism which mean that we cannot treat the Synoptic outline of the ministry as a chronologically reliable framework (and I have no desire to put a fundamental question-mark against that, although I believe that some deductions about the course of his ministry are still possible, and that a continuing effort to make the right ones is still called for); it is also due to the existentialist understanding of the Gospel material which sees the living Christ confronting us in every *perikope* so that, in Heinz Zahrnt's words "evidently the smallest unit of the tradition, the shortest scene and the briefest saying comprehend within themselves and reflect the totality of the person and the mission of Jesus"[32]—a statement which seems as questionable to some scholars as it does evident to others.[33]

But this lack of temporal or historical *depth* in the type of portrait of Jesus of which we have been speaking is also due in some measure to the use of the criterion of dissimilarity, and in particular to its use in connection with Jesus' death and his approach to his death. Partly because the death of Jesus is at the centre of the Christian proclamation, and his attitude and approach to his death very close to that centre (in the estimation of many), all the admittedly scanty material relating to that approach is suspect. In particular is this so because the prophecies of suffering and death in the Synoptic Gospels have obviously been influenced by the actual events and can all too easily be dismissed as nothing but *vaticinia ex eventu;* because the last journey to Jerusalem as an historical datum is heavily overlaid with theological motifs (and not only in Luke); because the other sayings which are relevant to the suffering of the Son of Man come under the kind of suspicion that attaches to all Son of Man sayings—especially since no "suffering Son of Man" sayings appear in Q. But I do not see how any assessment of the historical Jesus which is seeking to go further than Bultmann's can afford to ignore the question of Jesus' attitude to and approach to his death; and this not only for obvious theological reasons but for the very adequate historical reason that his death is the clue to the meaning of his life.[34] That statement may seem hopelessly ambiguous but can and must be defended as a statement with at least an important historical element. Wellhausen was hardly exaggerating when he said that without his death Jesus would not have become historical at all,[35] and without some assessment of his attitude to his death no understanding of his purpose could even begin to be adequate. Julius Schniewind, who in his day contributed a great deal to the proper understanding of the methods of Synoptic criticism, was entirely right to take very seriously the problem, for example, of the historicity of the Gethsemane narrative, just as we have also to take seriously the work of those writers like S. G. F. Brandon and Joel Carmichael who propound novel theories about the last days in Jerusalem and the political affiliations and aims of Jesus. We cannot discuss these problems here; I can only register my conviction that they are problems both for faith and for history, and my disagreement with those scholars who would deny this.[36] This of course is not to assert that Jesus must have seen in his own approaching death the same kind of significance that the Church has since found in it. Historical findings about Jesus' attitude to his impending death (meagre as these may be), and about the causes and circumstances of it are constantly needed to throw light on, to call in question, and to make specific the findings of the theologians. We see this happening, for example, at the present time in the debate within the Roman Catholic Church about Jewish responsibility for Jesus' death and, in a different realm, in Eduard Schweizer's study of discipleship.[37]

5. CONCLUSION

Here we may seem to have moved a long way beyond the discussion of those criteria of historicity which are our professed theme. It is therefore time to draw a few conclusions:

a. The so-called "criterion of dissimilarity" by which genuine material relating to Jesus is isolated can only be regarded as one among a number of heuristic criteria. It has a considerable usefulness in relation to individual sayings, sections of narrative, and characteristics of the teaching and action of Jesus, but it must be used alongside other criteria of different kinds, and it cannot be used as the basic primary tool of criticism or as the main method of establishing anything like a portrait of Jesus.

It may produce a critically assured *minimum*, but it cannot be said to produce an adequate historical *core*.

b. It follows that to use the criterion of dissimilarity to isolate "authentic Jesus-material" and *then* the criterion of coherence to build up a more adequate picture is much too simple as an overall rule. It may work in certain circumstances; but many other considerations will always enter in.

c. The criterion of coherence is extremely difficult to apply. Thus R. H. Fuller writes:

> . . . a saying like "The law and the prophets were until John" (Luke 16.16, Q) is authentic, because it squares with Jesus' message that the Reign of God has drawn near, whereas the saying, "Think not that I have come to abolish the law and the prophets" (Matt. 5.17), being inconsistent with Jesus' central message, will be a re-Judaization of the Jesus tradition.[38]

But this is altogether too easy. Does this interpretation of Luke 16.16 imply the correct understanding of Jesus' proclamation of the Kingdom and his relation to John?[39] And is Matthew 5.17 inconsistent with Jesus' central message? W. D. Davies, in a careful study, comes to a different conclusion.[40] The issue of coherence or consistency is never easily settled and, as was suggested above, when the test of coherence is applied after the test of dissimilarity as a matter of principle any errors in the results produced by the latter test will be compounded.

d. There is no way of avoiding the elaboration of hypotheses which must seek to cover as much of the evidence as possible, and in this process the factors leading to such elaboration and development as took place in the early tradition must be described and tested as rigorously as any others. Of course the elaboration of overall hypotheses and the isolation of a core of genuine material are not mutually exclusive activities; but the laying of stress on one or the other may indicate deeper differences of approach to the whole business of research into Christian beginnings—and that leads me to the very tentative thoughts which follow in the final section of this paper.

e. Much fuller comparison is needed of the methods and criteria which we have been discussing with those used by secular historians. Works like T. A. Roberts' *History and Christian Apologetic* have not received enough attention in this connection. For example, the use which the historian makes of unintentional data —evidence which historical sources "let out" accidentally, on matters not directly related to the author's intention—is closely related to the use of the criterion of dissimilarity; but arguments of this kind from unintentional data are not common among New Testament scholars. C. F. D. Moule, *The Phenomenon of the New Testament,* is a shining exception (see especially chapter iv). One suspects that secular historians would find many New Testament scholars unduly credulous in some directions and unduly sceptical in others.

2

1. COHERENCE AND CORRESPONDENCE

In commenting on what has been called the criterion of coherence I have suggested that (while the idea may be reasonably clear) the criterion is a very difficult one to apply. But there is another kind of coherence which has been invoked in connection with the inquiry into the nature of historical investigation as such. We are not here concerned with the attempt to understand the teaching or the life of Jesus as a coherent whole, but with a different use of a "coherence test" which is relevant to the interpretation of the findings of traditio-historical criticism.

We recall the long and indecisive debate among philosophers between the coherence theory of truth, naturally allied to epistemological idealism, and the correspondence theory espoused by the realists. Both theories have been applied to the study of history. According to the coherence theory, very roughtly speaking, the study of history consists in the elaboration of hypotheses which will be consistent both within themselves and, ultimately, with all other historical—and indeed all other—knowledge. Historical truth consists, not in correspondence between the propositions of history and historical fact, but in the relations between historical propositions. There are degrees of truth as there are degrees of coherence, and no one theory can claim to be finally true or false, for there are no hard, atomic facts for it to correspond to; facts, indeed, it is often argued by those who advocate this way of thinking, are already interpretations, hypotheses in embryo. The Achilles heel of the coherence theories, in the study of history as in knowledge of the external world, tends to be that they cannot account adequately for the given element in experience, and that they provide no final criterion for distinguishing between theories or hypotheses which appear to be equally coherent although mutually contradictory. The correspondence theories, on the other hand, maintain that there are and must be such things as facts to which propositions must correspond if they are to be true; and their Achilles heel tends to be, in the study of history as in knowledge of the external world, that there is no direct alternative way of knowing the facts (supposing such to exist) by which one can test whether or not the propositions made about the facts do correspond with them. And if this difficulty—the difficulty of representative theories of perception—can be overcome, there is still the difficulty, so far as history is concerned, that it is extremely hard to posit any fixed core or body of fact to which historical judgements must correspond.

This debate is not irrelevant to the search for criteria which we have been discussing. It may well be the case that neither the coherence nor the correspondence theory is adequate to describe the philosophical basis of the inquiry we call history, and that a synthesis of the two is necessary.[41] I suggest, as a very rough and tentative analysis of one aspect of the recent search for criteria in relation to the historical Jesus, something like the following:

Different as it is in its presuppositions from the whole co-herence—correspondence debate just referred to, the modern continental and American debate about the historical Jesus can to some extent be analysed in these somewhat Anglo-Saxon terms. The underlying philosophy and understanding of history, derived in the main from Dilthey and Heidegger, is from this point of view in its final effects unambiguously idealist. This is often concealed from us by the many obvious contrasts between the philosophy of existence and, say, the absolute idealism of a thinker like F. H. Bradley, for whom the historical events at the basis of Christianity were no more than incidental illustrations of universal truths of reason.[42] But when, as for Heidegger (if I understand him at all), history is not primarily concerned with the world of events and objects understood as causally related but with the repeatable possibilities of authentic existence for man, whose Being (*Dasein*) cannot be objectified, then in fact the criterion of *Geschichtlichkeit* ("historicality") becomes the possibility of such authentic existence, and the doctrine of man's selfhood determines what is significant in the past. This is ideal-ist in the sense that the life of the "experiencing subject" is what is truly significant, and in dealing with it we are dealing with that which determines the meaning of historical existence, past, present and future.[43] The Christian, or rather the Protestant, correlate of this view is very simply summed up in Kähler's statement that "the real Christ is the preached Christ". The historical Jesus becomes the Christ for us in the kerygma: but the conditions of the kerygma's being acceptable or intelligible reside within the doctrine of the self and the doctrine of man.

If this very bald statement, or anything like it, is at all accurate, then we can see how questions of historical truth are here judged by a rather special kind of coherence test. If history is concerned with the repeatable possibilities of authentic existence for man, or in Christian terms with the ever-renewed actualization of the kerygma, that is to say that historical truth is attainable when I encounter the selfhood of past figures, individual or collective, in a way that is coherent with my own self-understanding and with the documentary or other evidence. Thus the whole key to historical understanding rests in the resolution of the problem of different self-understandings, and in particular for our purposes the urgent problem of the relation between what we may call ancient, pre-scientific or "pre-secular", and modern, scientific understandings of the self and its place in the world.

But the use of the word "coherence" here may seem very misleading. For most exponents of the way of thinking of which I am speaking a vital element in the whole picture is the concept of encounter; the ancient text is not only a challenge to my understanding but to my self-understanding. It comes at me from the outside and demands that I reassess my own position; it must have existential significance for me if it is to have historical (i.e., *geschichtlich*) meaning; "it interprets me", we are told (whatever exactly that means), rather than my interpreting it. As with the text, so with the central figure with whom the text confronts me, Jesus Christ. Surely here, rather than formulating a hypothesis which will be coherent with itself and with other tenable and related hypotheses, I am thinking of an external reality which confronts me; the philosophical presupposition is "realist" rather than "idealist". It is just here that ambiguity arises, an ambiguity which is very relevant to our theme.

It is in confrontation with the ancient text, with the kerygma, with Jesus, that my own self-understanding is worked out; but in doing this I formulate "what Christ means for me" in terms which make sense for me today, and in this I am in the same position as those early Christians whose formulations come to me directly, and those still earlier original apostolic witnesses whose

31

formulations I can deduce, from the New Testament evidence. So, if I can overcome the problem of different "self-understandings" already mentioned, although these men of long ago are in some senses "external" to me, they share with me in a common Being (*Dasein*) which is common just insofar as it cannot be objectified, externalized, treated as a phenomenon in the impersonal world of cause and effect. Thus we build up a whole world of response-situations—and, to change the language for a moment, a world of "churchly memories"—which on the one hand is secure from some of the dangers of historical contingency and uncertainty, but on the other claims to take the historical seriously because only that which deals with the authentic life of man in response to his neighbours and to God is truly "historical". But ever and anon comes the fear that this world of challenge and response is simply an inner world with no sure link in content either to the transcendent reality of God or to the contingent, and therefore awkward, but external and in the end unavoidable world of "objective" historical process. In regard to the reality of God, Gogarten, Bultmann, and other modern theologians who have sat at the feet of the existentialists, have sought to overcome some of the difficulties of traditional theism by getting away from the whole "subject-object" frame of reference and positing another model for encounter with the Divine; how far they have been successful is a question which would take us too far afield. They have sought to do the same with regard to historical knowledge, and this is part of the reason why Bultmann dislikes the whole "new quest" of the historical Jesus. For the "new quest" seems to him to be reverting, albeit in a new way, to the bad old practice of establishing the certainty of the Christian proclamation on the very uncertain basis of the picture of Jesus given by historical research. Not only is this to build your house upon the sand, because the picture of the historical Jesus given by modern research is always changing; it is also, in the terms we have been using, to try to establish a *correspondence* between the picture of Jesus we get from our historical research and the "real Jesus", Jesus as he actually was (and therefore presumably is). And this you cannot do, because there is no alternative means of guaranteeing that this correspondence really exists. Bultmann of course does not use that language; but some of what he says can, I think, be translated in that way.

32

We may put the matter like this. Whatever its avowed aims, the new quest has tended to be a quest for the historical Jesus who is not simply the "faith-image" of the early Christians; who therefore in some way stands outside the "inner world" we have been describing. Some forms of the quest have attempted to by-pass the kerygma in order to get there (as in J. M. Robinson's *A New Quest of the Historical Jesus*); but this suffers from the difficulty that we are still within the "inner world" of existential selfhood, about which the doubts expressed above still hold. In any case it is extremely doubtful whether the methods and criteria of historical research can enable us to reach that "inner existential selfhood" which they are claimed to reach. So, for example, the project of J. M. Robinson falls a comparatively easy victim to criticisms of the type brought forward by Van A. Harvey in his recent book.[44] Other forms of the quest attempt to go "through" rather than "past" the kerygma—but some of the same difficulties still hold. In any case, the criterion of dissimilarity is being used in an attempt to establish those features of Jesus' words and deeds which are so distinctive that they could not have come from the reflection and proclamation of the earliest witnesses in their (of course legitimate) glorification of their Risen Lord.[45] But in this theologico-philosophical context the traditio-historical techniques are in danger of becoming something much more than techniques; they are becoming metaphysical weapons. What could not have been invented by the earliest witnesses is what came *ab extra* from Jesus himself; so too it comes to us, and confronts us with his living reality, his sovereignty, himself; and we scarcely notice that the historical Jesus, rediscovered by certain historical and therefore always provisional techniques, has virtually become the transcendent ground of our faith, not *as mediated by* but *instead of* the Christ of the apostolic witness. The early Christian witnesses and the Christ they preach stand within what may be called the "ideal circle": the historical Jesus stands outside it, and the guarantee that he does so is derived, in part at least, from the method of historical research which concentrates on what cannot have come from within the early Christian witness and must therefore come from the historical Jesus. It is almost as if an essentially idealist philosophy of history were being buttressed by a kind of superimposed realist dogma; if it is true, as was suggested above, that elements of both a "coherence" and a "correspondence" theory of truth are required in any satisfactory philosophy of history it seems doubtful whether the blending should be done in this way.

Sometimes, however, the tendency and the implicit assumptions are quite different. To that I shall refer later. Meantime, it must of course be admitted that what has been said does not correspond to any explicit intention on the part of any particular author, and is in any case an over-simplification of an extraordinarily complex issue. To many it must seem far worse, nothing less than a gross caricature. What I am suggesting is that since the preached Christ of the early kerygma is sometimes implicitly, even subconsciously, treated as an ideal construction within the realm of the "ideal/existential", the real, that is in this case the historical, Jesus who is properly speaking *extra nos* must be validated to us by methods which bypass or "pierce through" the ideal construction; and in this process the criterion of dissimilarity and other criteria which isolate what cannot have come from the early Church, become tools which perform a double function. They establish the lineaments of the picture of the historical Jesus and hence demonstrate a continuity and *coherence* (in spite of difference) between his message and that of the early Church; but because they are also held to establish what cannot have taken its origin in the early kerygma they come to be treated as the guarantee of the *correspondence* between the picture we have of Jesus today and what he really was (and therefore presumably is), the means of passage from the ideal to the real. Thus they are in effect providing not only an historical but a metaphysical validation of the kerygma. This is still true in its own sphere even when we admit that factors of faith enter in from the start, and that no historical interpretation and no criterion of historical explanation could ever validate the kerygma by themselves.

Perhaps we may sum up thus far, and restate our point, like this. The terms in which modern study of the New Testament is carried on often force us to distinguish between the "Christ of faith" and the "Jesus of history" and thus lead us to suppose that we can treat them as separable figures or entities. Both phrases, the "Christ of faith" and the "Jesus of history", can of course refer either to the picture or concept or image of Christ that we have "in our minds" or to the real Christ Jesus "outside our minds"—Christ as he really is (and was and will be), Jesus as he really was (and is and will be). It may well be misleading to treat these two entities—our image of Christ and Christ as he really is or was—as separable, just as it often is misleading to treat the Christ of faith and the Jesus of history as separable. But these are distinctions that, given the problems of today, we all seem forced to make implicitly or explicitly, in one way or another.

Now sometimes it happens that we tend to treat the "Christ of faith" as an ideal construction—"in our minds", as it were —whereas we regard the Jesus of history as the real Jesus who lived and died and rose again, and so the perfectly justifiable effort to see Jesus as he really was becomes the unjustifiable attempt to find the main or even the sole validation of our picture of Christ by means of historical argument, to pass from the ideal to the real by means of our criteria of historicity—and against this Bultmann has entered a perfectly proper warning. It is with that danger that we have been mainly concerned in the preceding paragraphs. Sometimes, however, the opposite process occurs. We treat the "Christ of faith", or the Christ of the Church's memory, as the "real Christ" and the Jesus of history as no more than an inferred figure who must always remain for us simply what our changing and therefore unreliable picture of him can give us—an image which corresponds more or less accurately to the ultimately inaccessible historical reality. It is because he is assumed to maintain an attitude of this kind that Bultmann has often, and perhaps rightly, been criticized.

To adopt, perhaps unwittingly, either of the two contrasting attitudes mentioned in the last two paragraphs is to distort and oversimplify the issues. We may see something of how that is so if we look briefly at some of the views of two recent writers, Ernst Käsemann and John Knox. This we shall do in the following sections. But again it must be stressed that the above characterization of the issues is itself much over-simplified. For example, we have spoken above of the "picture or concept or image" of Christ that we have in our minds: such language might suggest that visual metaphors are always the best ones to use in dealing with these matters, and this, it might be said, automatically rules out the possibility of speaking adequately about the impact that Christ makes upon us. We cannot enter into such matters here, and I must content myself with saying that the language here used while obviously inadequate in some respects does seem to provide one possible way of describing the issues with which we are concerned. It must also be stressed once more that what has been written above is an attempt, not to analyse any single author's procedures, but rather to give a warning about what is apt to happen when people carry on arguments about history and faith without thinking carefully enough about the presuppositions which they are using.

2. THE EARTHLY JESUS AND THE CHRIST OF FAITH

When Bultmann criticized the "new quest" as an attempt to legitimate the kerygma by means of historical research Ernst Käsemann turned the criticism aside by insisting that that was not what was at issue. What was at issue was the primarily historical question whether the earthly Jesus did in fact act as a criterion of the New Testament kerygma (or of legitimate proclamation) and how far that was the case.[46] In that formulation of the issue, which was of great importance, when Käsemann spoke of "the earthly Jesus", he presumably meant "the tradition about the earthly Jesus" or "the memory of the earthly Jesus". But perhaps in fact he meant more than that; as we shall see. Meantime, we can detect the importance of Käsemann's formulation in this way. If we begin with the historical question about the importance which the figure of the earthly Jesus had and has for Christian faith, we may avoid at least some of the difficulties referred to above. Instead of working backwards from the kerygma or from the Christ of faith to the historical Jesus, we shall rather attempt to study the impact made by Jesus, his life, death, and resurrection, and the impact he still makes, as an historical whole. The ambiguous and unsatisfactory concepts of the kerygma and the "Christ-event" will tend to disappear and something more closely related to Jesus himself may emerge to take their place.[47] To study what all this might involve would take us far beyond the limits of our subject. But we must at least notice that in this kind of context the criteria of authenticity used by traditio-historical criticism take on a different significance. They are no longer essentially means by which we try to isolate what cannot have come from the early Church so much as methods by which we detect aspects of the impact which Jesus made upon his contemporaries and followers.

That may seem a false antithesis; surely they are the one thing by being the other. But there is a change of emphasis, however slight, which is important. In fact the aim in view will no longer be a quest of the historical Jesus so much as an elucidation of the way in which Jesus Christ has always from the days of his flesh confronted those who have had knowledge of him—knowledge, indeed, in which the strands of "history" and of "faith" are sorely difficult to disentangle—and bear witness to him. We are no longer to accept a picture—the Christ of faith—as datum and seek to work back to the historical Jesus, or to accept some picture of the historical Jesus as datum and work forwards from it. Nor are we to begin with a community experience and seek to ask "what must the reality have been like to produce that experience?" in such a way that all we reach is an inferred figure whose characteristics, deeds, and words provide a sufficient occasion and explanation for the growth of the early Christian proclamation and theology. Rather we shall start by refusing to accept that the historical Jesus and the Christ of faith must necessarily be separable *Gestalten* at all, and we shall make use of the techniques of traditio-historical criticism to establish certain things about the earthly Jesus and other things about the early tradition without assuming that our picture of the one will ever become the controlling factor in establishing our picture of the other; so that we shall not expect to form an isolated portrait of the historical Jesus any more than we can form a definitive single portrait by combining what the four, or the first three, Gospels tell us. Further, we shall be constantly on our guard against any covert metaphysico-historical assumption about the kind or degree of reality which our techniques can establish. In particular, we must recognize that all forms of language about establishing pictures or portraits contain concealed epistemological assumptions; and so may the other form of language we have been using, about the impact which Jesus made and makes upon his people.

Whether the path followed by Käsemann since he wrote the essay referred to has been in any way like that just sketched may emerge from a study of his recent short book *Jesus Means Freedom*. This is not so much technical New Testament scholarship as a polemical tract for the German situation. My intention here is not to endorse, and certainly not to deprecate the force of, the many pungent things he has to say, many of which have considerable relevance to the British scene. But it is worth noticing one or two things about the ground from which he launches his attack. He begins, not with anything that could be called a rounded portrait of the historical Jesus, but with certain things which (he believes) can be said with full confidence about the man Jesus was and the impact he made. From that starting-point he expounds large areas of the New Testament, not explicitly testing what they have to say against what he has found about Jesus, but rather seeking to exhibit how certain characteristic themes run through them all. His theme is Christian freedom, but other themes could be handled in the same way. The Apostolic witness in the New Testament, he argues as he has done before,[48] is as much a witness to misunderstandings as it is a witness to a true apprehension of Jesus and the Gospel of the Crucified and Risen Lord.

> The pages of the New Testament [he concludes] have shown us that Jesus' sovereignty is refracted in the most varied ways on earth, and that we are able to grasp it and translate it into action only fragmentarily according to the existing situation. The Lord is more than the disciple—otherwise he would not remain our Lord. What we understand and achieve is patchwork, even under the power of the Holy Spirit, and is clouded by weakness, foolishness, and all earthly characteristics.[49]

So it was in the days of the New Testament, and so it always has been and is today. But we must not suppose that the New Testament witnesses are themselves in any way the villains of this piece. They are for the most part fighting a valiant battle in the varying circumstances which their writings reveal. (Käsemann's analysis of those circumstances may at times be questionable, but that is not the point here.) That is true, for example, of the Pastoral Epistles, where it was

> . . . not so much a question, as Dibelius thought, of turning the Church into a bourgeois society, although it may seem so to us. It was really a matter of stabilizing the conditions in a chaotic environment. We cannot deny the greatest respect to this undertaking, for the procedure that was followed was

appropriate, and what was appropriate in the Church's organization might well coincide with what was pleasing to God. . . It is no trifling matter when, in a disintegrating world, the Christian community achieves and maintains order, and through its mere presence calls to mind the good will of the Creator.[50]

I quote this passage merely in order to dispel any notion that this book is simply radical polemic against *status quo* in the Church, or that it fails to take seriously even the less promising parts of the New Testament. But it remains broadly true—and this is the point for us—that the historical Jesus, crucified indeed and risen, rather than any formulated kerygma or experience of the early community, is what holds the whole account together. The point of view is determinedly "realist", and this Jesus, Käsemann says, was a "liberal".

We need not delay over what is meant by that term, or the reasons for its use here, beyond illustrating something of its meaning by one more quotation:

He was a "liberal", because in the name of God and in the power of the Holy Spirit he interpreted and appraised Moses, the Scriptures, and dogmatics from the point of view of love, and thereby allowed devout people to remain human and even reasonable. Anyone who maintains the "true God" over against this liberal attitude may see that he is not sacrificing the real Jesus to an idol of his imagination and thereby destroying the basis of all Christian faith. For without this real Jesus we do not acknowledge any faith as Christian, even if it appeals to the Trinity and the resurrection of the dead at the same time.[51]

It is not our task to assess the truth of what is here said (the full understanding of which demands some awareness of the situation to which it is addressed); our point is that this "real Jesus" is the Jesus whom the Gospels, interpreted by historical criticism, show to us, and whom the Epistles, interpreted likewise, also show, if indirectly. Käsemann, like Bornkamm in *Jesus of Nazareth*, feels able to draw widely on the Synoptic material as giving a reliable and living picture of the historical Jesus, shining through the theologies or other interests of their several authors. This "real

Jesus" acts as judge and criterion for all true faith against excesses of imagination, perversions of dogma, and all manner of other dangers. This "real Jesus" stands out all the more clearly because the canons of historical criticism have enabled us to see certain features of what he was (and is) with greater clarity than would otherwise have been possible.

Is this to identify the "real Jesus" (Jesus as he was—and is, the same yesterday, today and for ever?) illegitimately with the historical Jesus (the figure of Jesus as he can be recovered by the changing techniques of historical research)? Is it in effect to turn this historical Jesus into the transcendent ground of our faith? Käsemann says that we speak of the great truths of the Christian faith (creation, God's people, the cross, resurrection, ascension, and judgement, the Church, canon, and sacraments)

> only as we can do so in the light of Jesus and through him. He must not sink in the profusion of so-called saving facts, nor even form their scaffolding. They must remain pointers to him, or reveal themselves through him. He is neither their product nor the code that holds them together, nor even their starting-point or centre. In that case he would cease to be our Lord and would become a place of wonders. . . . They speak of what he is doing and becoming to us, not of what he is taken to be, and did, and becomes apart from us. Because that is so, we cannot dispense with the earthly Jesus; he is our faith's unmistakable *vis-à-vis*.[52]

We notice here first of all the genuine existentialist emphasis; the earthly Jesus (was what he was and) is what he is not apart from us but in the light of what he is doing and becoming to us. Secondly, the use of the phrase "the earthly Jesus" presumably covers both the "real Jesus" and "the historical Jesus", as these phrases were used at the beginning of this paragraph; we may make the distinction in theory, but we cannot know any "real Jesus" apart from the "historical Jesus". His reality is known in his impact at all stages from the beginning of his ministry where he emerges into history until today. Thirdly, here and elsewhere there is no use of the phrase "the Christ of faith". This *Gestalt* has disappeared; and so has the kerygma, to all intents and purposes. So it seems as if, whatever other questions might be asked or criticisms made, the questions asked at the beginning of this paragraph must be answered with a "no", at least in this respect that the earthly Jesus and the Christ of faith are not being separated at all.

I spoke of the "genuine existentialist emphasis" in the passage quoted. But in this book there seems to be a subtle but important change of emphasis here. In his essay on "The Problem of the Historical Jesus" of 1953 Käsemann wrote, in typical existentialist fashion:

> Only that man is in genuine continuity with past history who allows it to place him in a new condition of responsibility. . . . In theological terms, this means that only in the decision between faith and unbelief can petrified history even of the life of Jesus become once again living history. This is why we only make contact with this life history of Jesus through the kerygma of the community.[53]

I have no reason to suppose that he would want to withdraw a single word of that statement. But in the new book there is a somewhat different thrust. It is not so much that we make the decision of faith in the light of which petrified history comes alive, but rather that the history of the earthly Jesus *is* living history —of course for those to whom he gives the gift of faith—and that he prescribes both what we are and how alone we can know him.

There is no laboured sense of the historical Jesus as an inferred entity, no obvious occasion and indeed little room for the Bultmannian concept of a *Vorverständnis*. The epistemological angle has changed.

Questions no doubt remain. Some will say that this is *Jesus*-centred rather than *Christo*centric (although I do not think that this would be altogether a fair criticism), others that the humanity of Jesus is too narrowly conceived, etc. In any case it is a change of emphasis rather than any sharp antithesis that is in question. For our purposes the fundamental point is that the criteria of traditio-historical criticism are no longer serving as "means of passage" back from the Christ of faith to the historical Jesus, from the ideal to the real, or from a known to an inferred figure. They are rather means of delineating more sharply some aspects of the given historical element in the Gospels (the phrase is unsatisfactory but it is hard to be more precise[54]), and indeed are one main factor in determining that the earthly Jesus, and the faith which we profess, relate to the whole world in which we have to live and not simply to the "inner human reality" which the dualism of the Bultmannian analysis of history had postulated as a self-existent realm. We are no longer using the criteria to give an historical rootedness to an inner world or to isolate an almost *in*humanly distinctive figure, but as the determinants of evidence that Jesus was a figure of whom we can discern certain vital things clearly, and that it was important in varying ways to his earliest disciples, and has been important ever since, to see him as he was. This is an historical procedure throughout; woven into the historical process, indeed, is the claim which he made and makes, the claim to which faith responds; but just because those claims are woven into the entire process, and there is no assumption of a methodological priority of the one over the other, the methods, that is the traditio-historical criteria, are left free to carry out their proper function, and to be criticizable as methods, rather than becoming the vehicles for half-concealed metaphysical presuppositions. This again is a relative matter, and the previous sentence is again doubtless an oversimplification. But I would hold to the judgement that in this method the dangers are less than they are with some of the others to which I have referred. The premisses and the conclusions of the argument of the book under discussion might be false; but the method has much to commend it.

3. THE MEMORY OF THE CHURCH AND CHRISTIAN FAITH

Some will say that Käsemann here uses the earthly Jesus, as he discerns him, to reduce the "whole Christ" of the tradition to a Christ who continually breaks and reforms, questions and renews it; so that the element of continuity and authority in that whole tradition is undervalued if not ignored. In that connection, and without trying to evaluate such a criticism, I would suggest that for Käsemann the words and deeds of Jesus which most directly communicate what he means for believers are those which we can confidently assign to the earthly Jesus, and that the christological formulations, Johannine "I am" sayings, Messianic titles, and the rest have as a main part of their function that of preserving his individual historical actuality (not of course in abstraction from his fate and his triumph) in its true import for faith. Contrast with that the following sentences from an author who acknowledges his debt to Professor John Knox:

> Knowledge of Jesus *as the Christ* is and must be mediated by the community of those who responded positively to the impact of Jesus upon them, and in responding interpreted it— sometimes by means of imagery and myth, sometimes by rewriting the history so as to bring out its deepest meaning. That is why the assertions of the New Testament which most directly communicate the saving knowledge of Christ are those which are most of all outside the scope of historical research, e.g., "God so loved the world that he gave his only Son, that whoever believes in him should not perish but have eternal life". That also is why the words of Jesus which most deeply communicate what he means for believers are those words which have arisen out of the Easter faith, and are the *least* likely to have been spoken by him in the days of his flesh, e.g., "Come to me, all who labour and are heavy-laden and I will give you rest", or, "For where two or three are gathered in my name, there am I in the midst of them".[55]

It is not my purpose to evaluate this author's whole position over against Käsemann's, but simply to point to the statement that there is a more direct and deep communication of what Jesus means for believers through those statements in which the strongest element of early Christian interpretation can be detected and to note that while this statement may well be true, when carefully formulated, it does not follow automatically from the author's preceding statement that knowledge of Jesus *as the Christ* (itself a phrase which carries large implications) is *mediated by* the early community.

Let us pass for a moment from that statement to the following further assertion:

> The reality which grasped the first Christian converts . . . consisted in the actual, concrete experience of belonging to an equally concrete and actual new community . . . with a highly distinctive style of life. . . . To be sure this community life was at every point grounded in and controlled by the "event" of Jesus Christ (the things he did, said and suffered), in which it

had its origin. But the only knowledge we can have of this event, and the only thing which made it the kind of event it was, lies in the concrete reality of that community life which came into being around it.[56]

That last sentence abounds in ambiguities; but leaving those aside we may paraphrase some aspects of the argument as follows: our knowledge of the earthly Jesus is indirect, mediated through the early community; but our knowledge of his saving significance, though mediated in the same way, is somehow more direct, since we have those statements of the early Church which tell us directly what he meant to them, and which are most outside the scope of historical research because they go furthest beyond the area within which historical statements can be made. But in the early Church (it seems to be implied) we have a concrete reality our knowledge of which is direct and unmediated (except insofar as *all* historical knowledge is in some senses indirect and mediated); it is therefore the ground of our knowledge of Jesus and his saving significance or Christhood. One suspects that there is an illegitimate passage here from the notion of an epistemological ground to that of an ontological ground; and that the Church is both these things is quite explicit in the works of John Knox; for example:

We need now to see that the Church's priority is not only epistemological, but actual; that the basic, objective, historical reality underneath, and presupposed in, all primitive confession —picture, kerygma, or whatever else—and the actual carrier of all the meanings being confessed was the early Church; and that, in consequence, the only adequate way to define the Event is to identify it with the Church's beginnings. . . . The historical Event to which all distinctively Christian faith returns is not an event antedating the Church, or in any sense or degree prior to it, but is the coming into existence of the Church itself.[57]

It is not for me to pick holes in this plausible but disastrously dangerous doctrine, but only to point out that if we define the "basic, objective, historical reality" as being the Church we shall certainly be unable to take the words and deeds of Jesus with full seriousness as impinging on that Church. Not only do we depend on the Church for our knowledge of them; they depend on the

Church, in some sense, for their very existence and meaning. (At times it seems that "existence" and "meaning" are identified in Knox's metaphysic.) What makes a coherent whole in history is true, and therefore real.

> Indeed, for all its integrity and intrinsic greatness, the career (of Jesus) has historical significance, even historical being, only because it belonged to the larger whole.[58]

The idealist circle is not broken, and life in the Church is secure.

What of the techniques and criteria of historical criticism in this context? They are no longer in danger of being used for isolating the portrait of Jesus in such a way that they become the guarantees of that portrait's reality for us in a more than historical sense—as we saw to be a danger in some forms of the new quest of the historical Jesus. They are rather "methods of passage" from the socio-historical reality which we can know to an inferred figure which we cannot know in the same direct way, and they help to establish a coherence between the words and deeds of Jesus and the faith of the Church. But of the various criteria the criterion of dissimilarity in particular does have a certain "realist-historical" tendency; it seeks to establish what made an impact upon those earliest Christians so strong that it cannot be assigned to their creativity—and what the crypto-idealism of much modern biblical scholarship fails to see is that its historical techniques stand in a certain tension with its philosophical presuppositions. This could be a creative tension, so long as we see that the traditio-historical techniques, if they are what they claim to be, give us historical knowledge just as direct (or indirect), knowledge of just the same epistemological *status*, as historical knowledge obtained in any other way. As soon as we make some covert metaphysical assumption about the status of our knowledge of the early Church, or of that Church as the "concrete reality" in which that knowledge "lies", over against other candidates for the honours, we shall find that we are distorting the historical techniques to serve these other ends. If the historical techniques are what they claim to be, they do not give us an inferred figure either superior or inferior in reality to the Christ of the Gospels. They tell us certain things, which we can now know with a degree of historical assurance related to the success of our methods, about that Jesus Christ—there is no

45

other. They do not serve to paint a different portrait from those of the Gospels, which could be set beside them; rather they bring out different features of the Gospel portraits with sharper clarity. Further, they have a genuine theological task in that they allow him to speak, to command, to comfort afresh to this generation. But they have this genuinely theological task only if and insofar as they are also treated as genuinely historical methods, provisional and changing but relevant to our day—all that we have so far been able to offer in this particular sphere of our obedience.

5. CONCLUSION

One point remains. This whole discussion up till now has paid no systematic attention to the problem of the relation, or better the identity-in-difference, between the earthly Jesus of the first century and the living Lord today. It has virtually ignored the central importance of the proclamation of the Resurrection. Here too the criteria of traditio-historical criticism have their part to play—not in any isolation from the Spirit or from tradition. Perhaps Käsemann can be criticized for using these criteria to establish too easy a *correspondence* between the earthly Jesus and the Christ who is always questioning and standing over his Church; and perhaps Knox and others can be criticized for using the same criteria to establish a *coherence* between the different parts of "the Event" which reduces the earthly Jesus to little more than an adequate occasion for the development of ecclesiastical life and tradition. It is hardly an accident that Käsemann and Knox would take different views about church history as well as about Christian origins. Perhaps these things depend more than we care to think on our social conditioning or our genetical make-up. But if you have come out to see more than a late Jewish prophet, more than a churchly figure, more than a portrait in two dimensions or the reflection of your inner will to believe, I suggest that Knox's way will never get you there. And Käsemann's might.

For Knox, in spite of his protestations to the contrary, does really "relegate Jesus to the background of the Christ-event"[59] at least in a metaphysical sense, and does so because like many others he cannot suffer the existential certainty of faith to be dependent on the changing and tentative results of historical research; whereas Käsemann seems now prepared to say that some historical findings are not for practical purposes changing or tentative but firmly established. This goes with the conviction that what has been firmly established is relevant and indeed essential for faith. The earthly Jesus of whom he speaks is not, in a number of passages in his writings, simply the picture of the earthly Jesus preserved by the early community but the living reality of the earthly Jesus, now crucified and risen, imposing himself upon the minds and hearts of his people. "Factors of faith" and "factors of history" are here indissoluble, and it can be argued that the historical realism of this approach is due to theological or psychological factors rather than to any careful consideration of the difficulties involved in the philosophies of many of his fellow-scholars. But the risk he takes in all this is the risk any Christian must take, and those who try to avoid it do no good in the end to the cause their apologetic motive seeks to serve.

Yet once more, and finally, is this not throwing far too much weight on the changing results of historical research? Was not the first part of this paper designed to show how shaky the methods in use, and therefore the results reached, often are? But if the methods are shaky, the moral is that they must be improved; and the further moral is that methods cannot be studied in isolation from historical, philosophical, and metaphysical assumptions which often modify them and make use of them in ways beyond those intended. Traditio-historical criticism has the task, among others, of showing us what manner of man Jesus was; and it has that task, *not* simply in order to prove that Jesus' character and mission are a sufficient ground for our explanations of the growth of the Christian faith, but in order to bring us face to face with the fact that if God truly entrusted himself to the changes and chances of the historical process (and most Christians do not really believe that he did) we can do the same. If we do, and only if we do, are we likely to encounter him afresh.

NOTES

1. "The Problem of the Historical Jesus", *Essays on New Testament Themes,* p. 34.

2. See especially J. Jeremias, "Characteristics of the *Ipsissima Vox Jesu*" in *The Prayers of Jesus,* pp. 108–115.

3. See H. K. McArthur, "Basic Issues; a Survey of recent Gospel research" in *Interpretation* 18 (1964), p. 48.

4. There is an analogous position in textual criticism; weight of numbers is no safe criterion for accepting a reading.

5. A striking example of the importance which this criterion in its formal aspect can have for modern scholars is found in Koester's important article ΓΝѠΜΑΙ ΔΙΑΦΟΡΟΙ in the *Harvard Theological Review* 57 (1956), pp. 293–4. Here, following Wendling and Bultmann, Koester argues on purely formal grounds that the saying found in Pap. Oxy. 1.6 and Thomas 87. 5–7 is more original than Mark 6.4 and its parallels ("Jesus said: No prophet is acceptable in his village, No physician heals those who know him"). On evidence of this kind together with certain conclusions about the identity of Judas, the brother of James and therefore of Jesus, with Thomas, and about the connection of the Thomas tradition with Edessa, Koester is prepared to suggest an independent Aramaic sayings-tradition connected with Edessa, a tradition of which we can still see many signs in the Gospel of Thomas and which gives us access to an original *Gattung* of the tradition of Jesus.

6. *Jesus the Messiah,* p. 129.

7. P. 35.

8. See e.g. H. Conzelmann in *RGG* [3] article on *Jesus Christus,* III, col. 623; R. H. Fuller, *The New Testament in Current Study,* pp. 40–1; *The Foundations of New Testament Christology,* p. 18; *A Critical Introduction to the New Testament,* pp. 94ff; G. Ebeling, *The Nature of Faith,* p. 52; E. Schweizer, *ZNW* 50, p. 201.

9. *The Foundations of New Testament Christology,* loc. cit.

10. F. G. Downing, *The Church and Jesus,* p. 113.

11. N. A. Dahl, "The Problem of the Historical Jesus" in *Kerygma and History*, ed. Braaten and Harrisville, p. 156.

12. See David Flusser in *HTR* 61 (April 1968), pp. 112–13.

13. *The New Testament and Rabbinic Judaism*, p. 388.

14. Cf. Fuller, *A Critical Introduction to the New Testament*, pp. 95, 98, who speaks of *consistency*.

15. *The Root of the Vine*, by Anton Fridrichsen and others, pp. 66–7. Cf. M. E. Dahl, *The Resurrection of the Body*, p. 85f.

16. *The Son of Man in Myth and History*, pp. 33ff. To give another example, H. Conzelmann has drawn attention to a very real problem, even if he exaggerates it, when he says that "there is no interconnection between the individual themes of his [Jesus'] teaching; that is, between his idea of God, his Eschatology, and his Ethics," (in Braaten and Harrisville, edd., *The Historical Jesus and the Kerygmatic Christ*, p. 65. But cf. also pp. 66ff). Cf. the same author's *Outline of the Theology of the New Testament*, p. 100.

17. Op. cit., p. 32.

18. This may be illustrated from an article by Howard M. Teeple, "The Origin of the Son of Man Christology" *JBL* lxxxiv (1965), p. 235. Almost every sentence in the last paragraph on that page is questionable; but no justification or arguments are offered.

19. "Gottesreich und Menschensohn in der Verkündigung Jesu" in *Festschrift für Günther Dehn* (ed. W. Schneemelcher), pp. 51–79; "Jesus und der Menschensohn," in *Z.Th.K.* 60 (1963), pp. 133–77.

20. *Z.Th.K.* 54 (1957), p. 281; *An Outline of the Theology of the New Testament*, pp. 131–7.

21. Op. cit. Cf. also H. Koester in *HTR* 61 (1968), p. 216.

22. There are some telling criticisms of the approach of the "Bultmann-Schule" and others to the Son of Man question in M. D. Hooker, *The Son of Man in Mark*, pp. 3–8, 79, 183–7; which is not to deny that their work has immensely advanced the study of the whole subject.

23. See *Z.Th.K.* 58 (1961), pp. 285–328; 63 (1966), pp. 1–32; R. Bultmann, *History of the Synoptic Tradition*, pp. 269, 306.

24. Op. cit., p. 39.

25. *A New Quest of the Historical Jesus,* p. 69.

26. There is a serious danger of theological "one-upmanship" here. The "radical" criticizes the "conservative" for being defensive because he is frightened of the theological consequences of denying that Jesus, e.g., claimed to be Messiah, and so creating a gap between Jesus and the Church. But the "radical" has his apologetic motives also; to see a large gap and find a new method of leaping over it is always a considerable theological accomplishment—or so it would appear. And if that is unfair (as it probably is) there are other apologetic motives in operation (as I have suggested).

27. I use the term "hermeneutical circle" in what I think was its original sense, and not in the way in which it is used in the contemporary theological discussion of hermeneutics.

28. *God was in Christ,* p. 20.

29. Note again: the "distinctive" equals the "characteristic". We need definitions!

30. *Jesus and Christian Origins,* pp. 176ff.

31. "The Method of the Life-of-Jesus Research" in *The Historical Jesus and the Kerygmatic Christ,* Braaten and Harrisville, edd., p. 65.

32. H. Zahrnt, *Es begann mit Jesus von Nazareth,* p. 67. Cf. Bornkamm, *Jesus of Nazareth,* p. 25.

33. Cf. S. Neill, *The Interpretation of the New Testament, 1861–1961,* p. 261.

34. Cf. Karl Barth, *The Epistle to the Romans,* p. 202.

35. *Einleitung in die drei ersten Evangelien,* p. 115; quoted by N. A. Dahl in Braaten and Harrisville, op. cit., p. 157.

36. See, e.g., Bultmann's most important essay published in English in Braaten and Harrisville, op. cit., pp. 15–42; John Knox, *The Death of Christ,* pp. 33–4; 124.

37. *Lordship and Discipleship,* chapters i–iii.

38. *A Critical Introduction to the New Testament,* p. 96.

39. See for example the comments on the latter subject in Van Harvey, *The Historian and the Believer,* pp. 189–90 (which also raise the important issue of chronology in the ministry of Jesus).

40. "Matthew 5.17, 18" in *Christian Origins and Judaism*, pp. 31–66.

41. W. H. Walsh, *An Introduction to Philosophy of History*, pp. 89–92.

42. The work of Karl Jaspers, among the philosophers, and Fritz Buri, among the theologians, seems however to show a number of points of similarity with Bradley. The idealism referred to in the text comes out clearly in the essay by Heinrich Ott in the volume edited by Braaten and Harrisville (n. 16).

43. The existentialist would of course claim that this concentration on the "inner life" as the determinant of significance is precisely what his doctrine is designed to overcome, by removing the old antithesis of "subject" and "object" and substituting a new model. But the result of this is only that the old antithesis pops up in a new form; either we have a dualism of "inner" and "outer", "being a self" and "being an object", or something of the kind, which is very difficult to resolve into a workable epistemological model, or there is a relapse into something not so very different from the old idealism.

44. This cannot be further documented here. See Harvey, *The Historian and the Believer*, chapter vi; and compare the criticisms of the "new quest" in Hugh Anderson, *Jesus and Christian Origins*, chapter iv.

45. This brief discussion ignores the question of the Spirit, which in any theological analysis is obviously central. But we can notice in passing that one way in which the question arises in relation to the principles and methods of traditio-historical criticism is this. It has been argued by scholars (e.g., E. Käsemann, "Sentences of Holy Law in the New Testament" in *New Testament Questions of Today*, pp. 66–81; German text in *New Testament Studies*, i, pp. 248–60) that a number of sayings in the Gospels which appear on the lips of Jesus are in fact the utterances of early Christian prophets speaking in the power of the Spirit, and that these utterances are or may be not only "true comments" on the significance of his mission and message but means of throwing further light on the historical Jesus himself. Such an analysis can of course also be applied to much in the Fourth Gospel, which is as a whole a reflection on this very problem and gives an explicit unfolding of it in the last discourse of chapters 14–16. The point to notice here, put very crudely, is that what the principles of traditio-historical criticism remove from the historical Jesus the doctrine of the Spirit restores to the "whole

Christ"; but we must then say that the mode of operation of the Spirit in the early Church is itself examinable by the methods of historical criticism, and that in that process not only historical criticism but theological evaluation, and indeed a readiness to see the work of the Spirit in the activity of scholarship itself, are involved. There is no easy way of isolating these factors and considerations, no simple order of priorities in application of methods.

46. "Blind Alleys in the 'Jesus of History' Controversy", *New Testament Questions of Today*, pp. 23–65, especially p. 47: "My own questioning is aimed at finding out whether the earthly Jesus is to be taken as the criterion of the kerygma and, if so, to what extent". Cf. p. 50: "The real problem is not how to give faith a historical foundation; it is how to use the critical method to separate the true message from falsifications of it, and to do this we need the help of the very One who was at that very time the historical Jesus, not by accident but by divine necessity". Käsemann's essential epistemological realism comes out at a number of points in this essay; not least in his criticism of Herbert Braun, pp. 37ff.

47. The word kerygma is ambiguous. It may mean "the message preached" or "the activity of preaching". As the former, it has been held to be an historically questionable entity: was there ever a single kerygma in any clear-cut sense? Many prefer in consequence to speak of kerygmata. But more important, the concept of the kerygma is ambiguous in that its relation to the "Christ of faith" is not simple. Christ is both content and agent of the kerygma; content of the message, and agent in and behind the activity of the preachers. Further, scholars sometimes write as if the kerygma and the historical Jesus were comparable entities. At first sight this is obviously a category error; what are comparable are the kerygma of Jesus and the kerygma of the early Church. Yet there may be relevant and important senses in which the kerygma takes the place of the historical Jesus. In a somewhat similar way we have to say that the "Christ of faith" is an ambiguous and unsatisfactory concept. Neither the kerygma nor the "Christ of faith" can be treated as a *Gestalt* or picture, a known or encountered entity or figure, without abstracting from essential elements in the complex reality to which they refer. We can have no picture of the "Christ of faith" in any kind of abstraction from what Jesus *was*; cf. the remarks of W. Pannenberg, *Jesus, God, and Man*, p. 28. To speak of a "Christ-event"

also has its dangers, some of which are shared by the concept of a "speech-event"; but to tackle them would take any man into very deep waters.

48. Cf. the same author's *Essays on New Testament Themes*, p. 102.

49. *Jesus Means Freedom*, p. 156. It is interesting to find the philosopher Hans Georg Gadamer making a similar point, in another context, where one aspect of post-Bultmannian hermeneutics is under criticism: "Versteht man unter Sinn eines Textes die *mens auctoris*, d.h. den 'tatsächlichen' Verständnishorizont des jeweiligen christlichen Schriftstellers, dann tut man den Autoren des Neuen Testamentes eine falsche Ehre an. Ihre Eigentliche Ehre dürfte gerade darin liegen, dass sie von etwas künden, das ihren eigenen Verständnishorizont übertrifft—auch wenn sie Johannes oder Paulus heissen". "Martin Heidegger und die Marburger Theologie" in *Zeit und Geschichte*, ed. Erich Dinkler, p. 489.

50. Käsemann, op. cit., pp. 96–7. Cf. p. 88, where the reference to Martin Dibelius is introduced.

51. Op. cit., p. 27.

52. Op. cit., p. 38.

53. *Essays on New Testament Themes*, op. cit., p. 24.

54. Cf. again Walsh, loc. cit.

55. T. G. A. Baker, *What is the New Testament?*, pp.93–4. A reference to the great "I am" sayings of the Fourth Gospel follows.

56. Op. cit., p. 20. We should notice that Baker glosses the term "event" in the passage quoted with the following footnote: "When the word 'event' is used in these chapters, it is intended to signify the total reality of the things which Jesus did and suffered, including in some sense their impact upon his earliest followers, both before and after his death—it therefore includes all that may be meant by 'resurrection' ".

57. *The Church and the Reality of Christ*, p. 22. "The Event" in this quotation means the same as "event" in Baker's usage.

58. Op. cit., p. 24. To study the similarities to, and differences from, Schleiermacher would throw light on the characteristic strengths and weaknesses of a good deal of modern "New Testament Theology", and not only on that of John Knox.

59. Op. cit., p. 21.